Dear Parent:
Your child's love of reading starts here!

Every child learns to read in a different way and at his or her own speed. Some go back and forth between reading levels and read favorite books again and again. Others read through each level in order. You can help your young reader improve and become more confident by encouraging his or her own interests and abilities. From books your child reads with you to the first books he or she reads alone, there are I Can Read Books for every stage of reading:

SHARED READING
Basic language, word repetition, and whimsical illustrations, ideal for sharing with your emergent reader

BEGINNING READING
Short sentences, familiar words, and simple concepts for children eager to read on their own

READING WITH HELP
Engaging stories, longer sentences, and language play for developing readers

READING ALONE
Complex plots, challenging vocabulary, and high-interest topics for the independent reader

ADVANCED READING
Short paragraphs, chapters, and exciting themes for the perfect bridge to chapter books

I Can Read Books have introduced children to the joy of reading since 1957. Featuring award-winning authors and illustrators and a fabulous cast of beloved characters, I Can Read Books set the standard for beginning readers.

A lifetime of discovery begins with the magical words "I Can Read!"

Visit www.icanread.com for information on enriching your child's reading experience.

Pinkalicious®
and Planet Pink

To Natalie
—V.K.

The author gratefully acknowledges
the artistic and editorial contributions of
Robert Masheris and Natalie Engel.

I Can Read Book® is a trademark of HarperCollins Publishers.

Pinkalicious and Planet Pink
Copyright © 2016 by Victoria Kann

PINKALICIOUS and all related logos and characters are trademarks of Victoria Kann. Used with permission.

Based on the HarperCollins book *Pinkalicious* written by
Victoria Kann and Elizabeth Kann, illustrated by Victoria Kann
All rights reserved. Manufactured in China.
No part of this book may be used or reproduced in any manner whatsoever without
written permission except in the case of brief quotations embodied in critical articles and reviews.
For information address HarperCollins Children's Books, a division of HarperCollins Publishers,
195 Broadway, New York, NY 10007.
www.icanread.com

Library of Congress Control Number: 2015940713

ISBN 978-0-06-241069-6 (trade bdg.) — ISBN 978-0-06-241068-9 (pbk.)

15 16 17 18 19 SCP 10 9 8 7 6 5 4 3 2 1
❖
First Edition

Pinkalicious

and Planet Pink

by Victoria Kann

In science class,

we learned about the planets.

They are the most amazing things

in the world.

I mean, in the universe!

"Every planet has
its own color," said Ms. Penny.
"Earth is blue and green.
Mars is a deep shade of red.
Venus is bright and milky white."

Ms. Penny showed us
something I'll never forget.
"There's even a pink planet," she said.
"Scientists just discovered it.
They don't know much about it yet."

For homework, we had to imagine
what the pink planet is like.
I had lots of ideas.
I know a thing or two
about pink places, after all.

PLANET PINK

Looks like a giant pink gumball.

Full of glittery stardust.

Home to fuzzy pink aliens

called Pinktonians.

I made a list.

Then I took out my pink paint

to make a picture of Planet Pink.

11

"There's no such thing
as a Pinktonian," Peter said later,
when I showed him my work.
"How do you know?" I said.
"Have you ever seen one?"

Peter thought it over.

"No," he replied.

"I don't think so."

Then he got very excited

at the thought of meeting an alien.

"Maybe Pinktonians

will come to Earth!" cried Peter.

"They'll fly down in their spaceship.

When they land, they'll say,

'Take me to Peter!'"

"No way," I said.

"If Pinktonians come to visit,

they'll want to meet me first.

I'm the most pinkerrific,

pink-loving person on the planet!"

"Maybe they'll like you so much,"
said Peter,
"they'll want to take you
back home with them."

"Ha-ha-ha," I said.

I knew Peter was just teasing.

That night, I had a weird dream.

A beam of light shone in my window.

I followed the bright pink footsteps.

There, in my yard,

was a huge pink spaceship

next to a tiny pink alien!

"Greetings," said the alien.

"I am a Pinktonian.

You may call me Pinky."

"Hello," I said shyly.

"We have come to take you
to Planet Pink," said Pinky.
"We hear you make great cupcakes.
They are our favorite food."

Pinky seemed nice,

and the offer was exciting.

But I didn't want to leave home.

The more I thought about it,

the more upset I got.

"Please don't make me go," I said.

"Nooooo, I want to stay here!"

Just then, I woke up.

I was safe and sound.

Except . . . something was odd.
There WAS a beam of light
coming through my window.
And all over the floor
were bright pink footprints!

I ran to get Peter.

"Wake up," I cried.

"There's a Pinktonian in my room!"

I told him my dream.

I showed him the clues.

Peter grabbed a flashlight.

I grabbed my wand.

We tiptoed around the room

looking for the alien.

Suddenly, we heard a scratch.

Then we heard a screech.

Then we saw something moving
under my bed.

"IT'S THE ALIEN!" we shouted.

Mommy and Daddy turned on
the lights.
"What's going on
in here?" they asked.
"There is an alien from Planet Pink
under my bed!" I cried.

Mommy started laughing.

There WAS a creature down there.

But instead of a pink alien,

it was a fuzzy white kitty!

"It's the neighbor's new cat,"
said Mommy.

"She must have climbed in the window
and stepped in your pink paint.
I'll wipe off her paws."

"We'll take her home tomorrow.
Good night, space explorers," said Daddy

I got under the covers.

The kitty snuggled up beside me.

I hadn't met a Pinktonian,

but I'd made a new friend.

As I drifted off to sleep,
I saw the kitten's collar.
Her name was Luna,
which is another word
for the moon!
How pinkaperfect!